The Art and Science of Teaching Composition

by
Dorit Winter

Published by:
The Association of Waldorf Schools of North America
3911 Bannister Road
Fair Oaks, CA 95628

The Art and Science of Teaching Composition

Author: Dorit Winter

Editor: David Mitchell

Proofreader: Nancy Jane

Cover photo: Camille Solyagua

ISBN # 1-888365-18-8

Curriculum Series

The Publications Committee of AWSNA is pleased to bring forward this publication as part of its Curriculum Series. The thoughts and ideas represented herein are solely those of the author and do not necessarily represent any implied criteria set by AWSNA. It is our intention to stimulate as much writing and thinking as possible about our curriculum, including diverse views. Please contact us with feedback on this publication as well as requests for future work.

David S. Mitchell
For the Publications Committee
AWSNA

Table of Contents

Introduction 1

Chapter 1 The Foundation of Writing 4

Chapter 2 Wonder 12

Chapter 3 Wish 30

Chapter 4 Surprise 39

Chapter 5 Conclusions 45

Postscript 49

Endnotes 50

INTRODUCTION

Although this book focuses on the seventh grade main lesson traditionally called, "Wish, Wonder and Surprise," it is intended for teachers of all grades. Using "Wish, Wonder and Surprise" as the source for my examples and my research, I have attempted to show how the seventh grade teacher can guide the children through a series of writing exercises that are as calibrated to meet the seventh grader as is the rest of the seventh grade curriculum. The method, however, of relating the teaching of composition to the essence of the developmental stage of a particular grade is applicable at any grade level.

Every Waldorf year is a transition from the one before to the one after. Every year of the Waldorf curriculum is the remedy for the discomfort of the transition. In seventh grade, nascent cognitive powers and critical thinking are emerging more and more. But something, too, is waning: acceptance of authority, assumption of the unity of self and world. These grow ever more tenuous, ever less certain. The entire seventh grade curriculum, with its *leitmotif* of emerging Renaissance faculties, steadies the children in their passage, a passage that can be particularly hard, because seventh graders shuttle wildly between contiguous realms of great contrast. This contrast is the theme of wish, wonder and surprise.

In their **content**, the writing exercises, the composition assignments as represented by the themes of "Wish, Wonder and Surprise," allow the children to find a new, more conscious relationship to soul states that in earlier childhood were natural habitats. In their **style**, their growing emphasis on precision and clarity, these same assignments guide the children's ripening capacity for articulation.

The **what** and **how** are the weft and warp which can be adjusted to meet the developmental needs of any grade. The writing tasks can be woven to fit the needs of the moment.

The sixth grade teacher may try to glean the essential soul mood of the sixth grade curriculum. Is it perhaps related to the balance of power and justice? Once alerted to the possibility of a particular inner quality, our reading of Rudolf Steiner, whose writing so often elucidates the soul and all its experiences, will provide us with ever deepening insights into the esoteric background of the soul mood we are investigating. Out of such research, the content for properly calibrated writing assignments will emerge.

In third, fourth and fifth grade our attention, as regards the children's writing, will focus on **what** they are describing. Of course we expect them to follow the rules they have learned — a sentence begins with a capital letter — but it would be premature to be overly analytical about **how** they express themselves. In sixth, seventh and eighth grades, the content, the **what**, has to be sustained more and more by confidence in technique, in the **how**, so that the writers' palettes give rise to sentences and thoughts of growing complexity. By the time the students are in high school, we can plumb ever more profound depths in our teenagers, by concentrating on **how** we, and the great writers, articulate them.

CHAPTER 1

THE FOUNDATION OF WRITING

Turning now to seventh grade, we find a unique main lesson, one that has moods of soul as its explicit content: wish, wonder and surprise. Why should moods of soul be part of a child's education? And why especially in seventh grade?

In the twelve year Waldorf curriculum of main lessons, seventh grade marks the far side of half way. A dividing line has been crossed; but if we turn around, we can still look back to a time of unalloyed childhood, when, to borrow an analogy from art history, the sky was still golden.

Up to the time of Giotto, the great forerunner of the Renaissance, the sky was painted in gold. Giotto, too, sometimes reverts to that golden sky, but most of the time he paints a blue sky. Giotto sees that the sky is blue; what he sees beneath this blue sky is illuminated by physical light, which gives his landscapes and the figures in them mass and contour; bodies have bulk beneath robes and cast shadows, and feet stand on the ground. All this Giotto sees with his outer eye. And he paints what he sees. That is Giotto's revolutionary achievement. After Giotto, the golden sky, beneath which the physical world appeared but hazily, recedes forever. This world, not the next, comes, ever more rapidly, ever more clearly, into focus. And yet, revolutionary though Giotto's blue sky is, it is still only a first delicate, diaphanous possibility, merely a thin membrane stretched between this world and the next, with angels in somewhat clumsy perspective poking through. Although it spreads a physical light, it illuminates a spiritual world. Substantial though his landscapes and his figures are, it is his inner vision that Giotto attends to: the life of St. Francis, the life of Christ. Indeed, compared to the realism achieved by artists of the high Renaissance, Giotto's work is crude. We are not yet under the deep blue sky of the Renaissance horizon toward which three-masted galleons will sail on their way to the New World. Giotto's other-worldly landscape is still relatively flat. Neither the painter nor the painted figures grasp the physical world in detail. Nor does that seem to be the goal. The eyes of the figures, for example, are physiologically inexact. Like the eyes of the painter, they are still focused on a landscape determined primarily by the spirit, instead of by laws of perspective. And yet, landscapes, figures, features, and expressions are poignantly individual, carefully observed.

Giotto lives in both worlds, the old, spiritually imbued world of glorious gold, and the newly seen world where the sky is blue. Although stealthy, anatomical investigations of cadavers are still centuries away, a divide has been crossed: the sky is blue, and the light from above is beginning to reveal the world in all its diversity.

So we might say the Waldorf curriculum is an attempt to illuminate the growing child's passage into the world with just the appropriate light, neither prematurely blue, not regressively gold. And seventh graders are at a particularly ticklish transition. For the seventh grader, the allure of the physical world is natural. It would not be right to keep budding adolescents in the realm of the golden sky. They are looking around, and we are pedagogical when we provide them with what is worth seeing, and discipline their dawning powers of observation. That is why physiology, chemistry, geometry, and perspective drawing are all introduced in seventh grade. The *science* in these subjects meets the students' natural scientific curiosity and allows them to objectify their own explorations of the world, as does the study of the Renaissance itself.

But the lure of today's physical world with all its materialism is extreme. Today you do not have to be Magellan to circumnavigate the globe; you need not be Galileo to investigate the moon. All you need is a computer served by the Internet. At the turn of our millennium, the alternative to the golden sky is far more dangerous than any *terra incognito,* for it is available, illusory and seductive. The monsters in the deep are real. Not just the insatiable astral body lurks at the edge of the known world of childhood, but the minutiae and false wonder of electronic wizardry wait to consume any abiding "visionary gleam."

The seventh grade teacher must find an *appropriate* balance between the students' growing desire for knowledge of the world and self, and the lingering gleam of childhood's gold, which is naturally, and unnaturally, slipping away. Part of that disappearance is healthy, but it is unhealthy when the inner light, that inner sanctum, is mindlessly blotted out, a fate suffered by even the littlest children in the culture of *Technopoly*[1].

Waldorf education attempts to preserve, *appropriately,* as much of the inner light for as long as possible, not because it wants to imprison children in childhood, but because if that child's innate, golden light is tended, strength of soul, strength of character, are cultivated for that child's entire adult life. That strengthening is only possible if we preserve without embalming, if our preservation not only allows growth and metamorphosis, but encourages it.

In seventh grade, then, we teachers must realize that the light breaking through the blue vault of heaven reveals the tangible, here-and-now physical world in the three-dimensional relief, which entails light and shadow, bulk, and the heaviness of weight. *At the same time* the preserve of innate inner light and inner life is, nevertheless, also still present. (By eighth grade we can objectify those phenomena in our study of black and white drawing.)

For seventh graders *do* still partake of light that is golden, but they will mightily resist expressing it. That is natural. Being pedagogical then means: getting them to express it, for what is articulated is strengthened. Through the art of pedagogy we strengthen what needs strengthening by devising *appropriate* ways for the youngster to experience *and express* the shy, vanishing inner life. We set a task which has enough "science" in it to satisfy the seventh grader's craving for the phenomena of the world without allowing him or her to succumb to superficial worldliness. If today we succeed in fostering the child's soul life, then, tomorrow, when the child is an adult, soul mood will become soul strength.

So when, for example, we teach chemistry in seventh grade, we must enliven the scientific method which we are emphasizing by creating conditions under which the seventh grader's inner life will also be touched by the phenomena. Let us, by all means, do our chemistry experiment *scientifically.* Let us observe *carefully.* Let us get beyond such sloppy observations of the burning of fur as, "Yuck!" or even, "It stinks!". Instead, let us carefully note the combustion process with as much detail as we can muster. What color is the smoke? What shape is the flame? What is the quality of the ash? Then let us write up the experiment *carefully*. Now let us write a composition about fire: its characteristics, its uses, its effects. Let us be sure to craft the composition *scientifically,* i.e., according to a plan, an outline, an objective structure, *with discipline.* Finally, out of all that hard scientific work, a poem may arise. But it, too, must have science: structure, rhythm, rhyme, as well as content. In fourth grade we might have allowed a free-for-all poem. But here in seventh grade the demands must be *scientific,* i.e., rigorous in form and method. Then we will have the students' interest, and we will get substantial and disciplined poems. Here are some that were written by seventh graders as part of their chemistry block:

FIRE

Hot and glowing, red and orange,
Shooting higher, burning fire!
In the darkness of the night
Flames protect from things of fright.
Used for cooking, heating, shelter
And for light.

Since the cave men lit their torches
Flaming fire burns and scorches,
Through the ages man has used
These fiery flames for good and bad.
Holy candles burning softly
Help to ease a heart that's sad.
– by Charles

WATER

Water in the dew,
Water in the stew.
Water it can cool,
When in the swimming pool.
Water, it can fall and rise,
So that it should be no surprise
That it really never dies.
Water is a vital thing
For life of even the highest king.
Without the water in our eye,
We'd never see the rainbow in the sky.
– by Erich

Both Erich and Charles were in my seventh grade class at the Rudolf Steiner School in New York City, where, in 1978, I taught this main lesson for the first time. Erich was a rascal, full of mischief, his hands perpetually busy with wires and bolts, his homework minimal, his attention span brief. Today he is a much-sought-after car mechanic. Did he ever write another poem? I don't know. But what a revelation for his teachers this poem was. What a revelation for his parents. What a revelation for Erich! Beneath the tumult of provocateur and amusement chief beat the golden heart of a noble philosopher. Once glimpsed, it was never forgotten.

As for Charles, I've lost track of him. But I do recall that though his artistic leanings were often not fully understood by his classmates, this poem aroused real admiration; it was so full of spark!

CHAPTER 2

WONDER

Both poems have a fine balance of blue and gold, of facts and *wonder.* For the seventh graders the facts were what the poems were about. For me, their teacher, the implicit mood was the real goal. The facts were not new to the students; they had experienced fire and rain before. But the attention, the *care* with which we observed these phenomena, the *mood* I strove to bring about through our scientific experiments, was a mood of care and wonder. It is likely that as they grow up, children will encounter the *facts* of the seventh grade curriculum anyway. But exercising the soul, by providing it with (surreptitious) opportunities for *wonder,* gives the growing youngster an inner sanctum where, in time, the spirit can lodge.

> Just as the sun's rays vivify everything living, so does reverence in the student vivify all feelings in the soul...feelings are for the soul, what food is for the body. If we give the body stones in place of bread, its activity will cease. It is the same with the soul. Veneration, homage, devotion are like nutriment making it healthy and strong, especially strong for the activity of cognition. ...The outer world, with all its phenomena, is filled with divine splendor, but we must have experienced the divine within ourselves before we can hope to discover it in our environment.[2]

These words do not pertain to seventh graders. They are meant for us, their teachers. But the principle holds. "Veneration, homage, devotion" strengthen the soul "for the activity of cognition."

Of course, esoteric knowledge is not the goal of the seventh grade curriculum. But what is true for the soul of the consciously seeking adult is true for the soul of the unconsciously seeking pre-adolescent. In both, "feelings are for the soul, what food is for the body." The teacher's task is to implement the right feelings, and the indication "Wish, Wonder and Surprise" may serve as a guidepost signaling that WISH, WONDER and SURPRISE are the right feelings.

Rudolf Steiner refers often to the need for the feeling of wonder in the adult, and in the child.

> Whenever you think of how a morse apparatus at one station is linked to another at another station, you are reminded of the miracle that makes the earth, the whole earth, into a mediator, taking the electric current as though into its care and duly delivering it at the next station. The earth itself mediates in this way. All the explanations that exist for this are hypothetical. But the important thing as regards our human attitude towards it is that we should be able ever and again to feel how miraculous this fact is, that we should not become blunted in our ability to grasp the processes of physics with our feelings. Then when we explain these things to the children, we shall find the mood that again and again allows us to return to the way we first took in a fact when we grasped it. Then when we explain a phenomenon of physics to a child who is full of wonder we shall ourself become children full of wonder. Such marvels are hidden in all things including the processes of physics that take place in the world.[3]

So wonder in the teacher invites wonder in the child. For the Waldorf teacher, anthroposophy itself is the wellspring of wonder, as the fundamental *condition* for attainment of higher knowledge already showed us. How fundamental this attitude of soul is, is further revealed in the 4th ("Positivity") and 5th ("Openness") of the so called "Six Basic Exercises," which are like soul conditioners, toning our capacity for wonder.

For Rudolf Steiner himself, wonder is a guiding principle, through which "the cognitional faculty is ripened."[4] Here he is, speaking about the human body:

> ...the manner in which these substances and forces [which exist in the wider mineral realm] interact in the human body, is the expression of wisdom and perfection in the structure. ... One can take any part of the human physical body as the subject for this contemplation, for instance the highest part of the upper thigh bone. This is not an amorphous massing of substance, but rather is joined together in the most artful manner, out of diminutive beams which run in different directions. No modern engineering skill could fit a bridge or something similar together with such wisdom. The bone is constructed in this wise fashion so that, through the arrangement of the small beams, the necessary carrying capacity for the support of the human torso can be attained with the least amount of substance. The least

> amount of matter is used in order to achieve the greatest possible effect in terms of force. In the face of such a "masterpiece of natural architecture," one can only become lost in admiration. No less can one admire the miraculous structure of the human brain or heart, or of the totality of the human physical body.[5]

Here is Rudolf Steiner, himself filled with wonder, providing us with a fount of wonder for ourselves (and, incidentally, for our seventh and eighth grade physiology classes).

Rudolf Steiner guides us toward an understanding of the importance of wonder for ourselves, and he gives us ways to strengthen our sense of wonder. It is up to us to give our students the means for experiencing wonder, for unlike us, they are not deliberately seeking and cultivating such an attitude.

In a world where the stroke of a computer key creates, destroys and recreates whole worlds in seconds, how can the "twinkling stars, the scudding clouds, the budding, sprouting blossoms" provoke wonder? The computer screen makes mockery of wonder, awe, reverence, veneration. Our children, and many of us, too, have been digitally impaired. S/he who takes the universe for granted, for whom wonder has atrophied, who not only can't "see the world in a grain of sand," but who also doesn't see the point of trying, has lost not just the capacity for wonder, but the imagination, too.

Fundamental to both wonder and imagination is observation. The poet's eye or the painter's eye conjures up great landscapes in precise detail without virtual reality. Such eyes are trained in observation. Therein lies the science of the art; therein lies the scientific method the seventh grader and the striving anthroposophist need to practice. In *Practical Training in Thought* we find that "Goethean Observation" is the basis for objective thinking.

> To the extent that we insert ourselves into the course of the world through observation of the events in the world, and receive these images into our thoughts with the greatest possible clarity, allowing them to work within us, to that extent do those members of our organism which are withdrawn from our consciousness [the reference here is to the astral body] become ever more intelligent.
>
> Time must be taken to observe things as though we were inside the things themselves with our thinking.

Such observation, if properly trained, develops into true imagination.

In our kindergartens and the early grades, we can still directly address the child's sense of wonder. For some children, it is a sense already badly wounded. Through the imagination it can be healed. The tales we tell our little children are wonderful. In fourth, fifth and sixth grades, we have to begin to evoke that sense of wonder less directly. By seventh grade, if we address the sense of wonder directly, we will be laughed out of the classroom. For the seventh grader is donning the heavy armor of adolescence, and the more complete it is, the more s/he fears exposure of the tender soul which still enjoys the golden sky. The golden sky is in the past for seventh graders; they are turned outward, toward the uncharted future. Any hint of inwardness makes them explosively uneasy, and rightly so, because *now* for the seventh grader is the dawning epoch of the consciousness soul. (As perhaps we might say that *now* for the eighth grader is the twentieth century, and *now* for the ninth grader is today, whereas for the tenth, eleventh and twelfth grader, more and more of tomorrow creeps in.) In that dawning, where the blue and the gold are both present, there are unexpected *new* joys. One such new joy is the discovery of the power of keen observation, whether in a chemistry experiment, a geometric proof or in a preliminary exercise for a writing assignment. For "WISH, WONDER and

SURPRISE" ought to be inwardly experienced activities, evoked by an active imagination through the means of written compositions; and the compositions that most *scientifically* evoke the inner mood of wonder through an outwardly oriented scientific method are based on exercises in observation.

Typically, this main lesson is given three weeks, one for each of the soul moods. As is probably clear by now, it seems not merely legitimate, but even preferable to deal first with WONDER. Though it comes second in the conventional name of this block, it is the first condition for all our striving.

Before continuing with some practical suggestions, a word about the name of this block. Do not call this block "WISH, WONDER AND SURPRISE." That would be like trying to lure the shy deer into the forest glade by shouting: hunters! traps! wolves! Much better to call this block "Creative Writing." (The designation, "Creative Writing" is unfortunately misleading. "Imaginative" or "individual" would be better terms than "creative" which, for most of today's world, implies the anything-goes ethic. But the conventional term "creative writing" covers the activity our seventh graders will engage in, so we might as well call it that, rather than coin one more Waldorfism.)

During your "warm-up" time (by seventh grade we should no longer be calling it "morning circle") introduce the new poem. Wordsworth's "My Heart Leaps Up" is a fine possibility; there is no shortage of poems filled with the mood of wonder. Beware of sentimentality. Find a text with more blue than gold. Remember that the "blue" may be in the context, the structure, or the elements of the poem, not just in the content. "Cargoes" by John Masefield, with its sturdy nouns, is another poem that comes to mind. Or something like: "Many are the world's wonders, but none more wonderful than man...." from *Antigone* by Sophocles, may also work, if you introduce it dramatically, giving a bit of its context in the great drama from which it comes.

You might want to start your main lesson by distributing some natural objects: leaves can be effective if setting and season are appropriate. Feathers, small crystals, special stones, sea shells are other possibilities. The children will wonder what it's all about. That's fine. Let the suspense build a bit. This kind of "wondering" is not the same as the WONDER we are after, but it is an important tool for the pedagogue/dramatist which every teacher must be. Now ask them to write a description of the object. Explain that at the end of 20 minutes you will collect all the objects and compositions, and then display the objects all together while reading aloud some of the compositions. Will the description identify the specific object? That is the goal. So the description must be very *exact.* Aha! *Scientific!* Of course, the more alike the objects, the harder this becomes. So you may have succeeded in surreptitiously giving your best writers very similar objects, while giving the weaker writers some clearly identifiable objects. For homework, you might give them a similar task, perhaps with an object they themselves have to discover.

In correcting their compositions, focus on the precision of the description. Of course, you have to correct the usual: spelling, punctuation, grammar, etc. But in evaluating the work, do not let that be the emphasis. Rather, consider how the object is approached, how the sentences follow each other, whether the vocabulary is specific enough. Can "brown" become "burnt sienna"; "small" become "the size of my thumb fingernail" or "$^{1}/_{2}$ inch by $^{1}/_{2}$ inch"? Can "look at" become "observe," "investigate," "examine"; or "stone" become "crystal," "quartz," or "rose quartz"? If we do not know the precise name of a thing, can we *research* it? Is the leaf from an oak tree? What kind of oak is it? Some reference books in your class room will enhance the *science* of the project. Such raising of vocabulary-consciousness can be part of your morning lesson. You cannot spend the entire main lesson writing. To begin with, twenty minutes or half an hour of concentrated work is as much as most seventh graders can manage. *Visual* or *Naming Dictionaries* provide endless treasures of precise nomenclature. (Needless to say, there will be students who get lost in the details; they will have to be pulled back to gain the wider perspective once again.)

This raises the frequently asked question of what to do during the rest of the main lesson, when the children are not writing. Writing is the order of the day, each day of this block, perhaps even twice a day, if we reckon the homework as well. However, since everything the children write has to be corrected by the teacher, and then by the student, whose corrections then need to be checked by the teacher again, the homework load ought to be distributed with the teacher's health and sanity in mind. Some teachers have found it practical to work on a play, or even on something more remote, like arithmetic, during the time when the children are not writing or working on their main lesson books. It might be advantageous however, to use that time for *writers' workshops* of various kinds. Once you have come up with that kind of *scientific* name for the activities, you have quite a broad range: vocabulary building activities of every conceivable sort (games you've invented, "research," work with suffixes, prefixes, synonyms, antonyms, etc.); lessons in composition structure, paragraph structure, sentence structure; exercises with tense, voice, mood; reading; drama, improvisations, skits.... anything appropriate to the enhancement of the writer's skills EXCEPT grammar as usual. Most children (and grown-ups, including teachers) have such an aversion to grammar, that it is best, just for now, to avoid grammatical terms and the usual approach. That doesn't mean you cannot devise discreet approaches to such grammatical necessities for the skillful writer as active and passive voice. It just means you have to find an approach that a *writer* might appreciate, an approach that comes out of the entire tenor of this block. For instance, if a student starts an observation exercise with a sentence like, "This shell was looked at for a long time by me," you have a good reason for pointing out why that is a weak beginning.

What will you do for the rest of the week? Well, presumably you have some sort of master plan you can adjust according to unfolding events. That plan might include:

- setting up the desks in a circle and placing an arrangement of still life (vase with flowers, etc.) in the center. Every child will have his or her own point of view to describe, and this should be obvious through the description, so great clarity with prepositions is required.

- describing a famous painting, preferably one that is action-packed. If John Constable were next door, would he be able to paint that jumping horse from a written description?
- looking through the window: landscape or cityscape depending on whether you are in a rural or urban setting. Can we describe the nuances of light and shadow? Catch the people walking along on the sidewalk? Would my cousin who lives in London and has never been here be able to see, hear, smell this view?
- taking the children into a park. Have them all describe the same scene, and/or let each student choose his or her own.
- a verbal portrait of a family member.
- a verbal portrait of a pet.
- and so on.

As these daily exercises are progressing, so are the "clean," corrected copies of the compositions. Unlined paper and suitable illustrations (NOT random decorations) might be encouraged.

The point, to reiterate, is to get the seventh graders to look *carefully.* Once you have managed to improve their observation skills and their ability to articulate their observations, you might want to read some gems of descriptive writing to them. (If you do this first, the clever students will try to be "copy cats," while the rest get discouraged.) John Muir, Henry David Thoreau, Rachel Carson, Annie Dillard, Lewis Thomas, John McPhee, for instance, are all fine nature writers.

Later, perhaps even after this main lesson block is over, you might read aloud to your class some accurately imagined landscapes, accurately imagined characters (Dickens!). For imagination is the result of careful observation. You can inspire your seventh graders to new heights of clear prose once you have fired them with the challenge of careful observations. In this way, you will be training the imagination, which is the basis of true thinking.

Here is a piece of fiction from a former seventh grader under the influence of *scientific observation.*

AT THE MOUTH OF A TIDAL CREEK

> As the tide slowly comes in, little minnows come with it, bringing screaming terns to the spot. Small sandpipers scuttle along the flats searching for sand bugs and worms. The sandbars reach far into the distance, with water lapping ever so lightly at their edges. Red, green, yellow and brown seaweed drifts with the current. Tiny hermit crabs hurry along the bottom

in search of food. In the sand, lavender and beach grass grow in abundance. Along the beach, horned larks scurry along on various errands.

Further up the creek , a green heron hunts in solitude, stalking fish and stabbing them to eat. In the water, amidst the sea grass, there are fiddler crabs running around and waving their oversized claws in the air. On the edge of the grass, green crabs and calico crabs scavenge for food.

– by Alexander

True, some of the adjectives are generic (small, red), but the details more than make up for that. This paragraph is evidence of an active inner eye. Alexander was interested in life at the edge of the sea; he knew the names of things. He also had a good ear and could compose his sentences into effective cadences. He had learned, in countless *writing workshop exercises,* how to vary the structure of his sentences, to use (perhaps too enthusiastically) the prepositional phrase. And when he wrote the paragraph his inner eye and his inner ear were engaged. Doesn't the boy's wonder speak through the details? The scene is imagined, but it is the result of careful, informed observation, which Alexander had learned to articulate.

Challenging the seventh graders with the goal of *scientific* observation of apparently unscientific things, events, situations, is, if properly structured, irresistible to our Renaissance crew. Their enthusiasm, not their cynicism, will flourish. Cynicism, the scourge of our youth, prevails when wonder is squashed. Our *writer's workshop* approach, on the other hand, gleans gold. We move from observation, to wonder, to enthusiasm, to learning. And some of what we learn, we may even retain.

Here is a short story, written at the end of eighth grade by a boy (yes, there were girls in this class, but I don't seem to have any of their papers any more) who had woken up to writing during the seventh grade. His story follows the outline we had developed through many exercises: setting, character, incident, resolution. It is an imagined story. Note the details.

A MOMENT ON A MOUNTAIN STREAM

Cold clear water sparkled over the rocks, while little silvery minnows darted around a pool in a trickling mountain stream. The sunlight flashing through the water made wave-like patterns on the rocky stream bed. About ten yards up stream a young pine tree bowed into the water, as if it were drinking, but as the breeze let up, the tree sprang out of the water, leaving a trail of pine needles floating down stream. Dead leaves bobbed up and down in the current and raced little twigs down stream. Along the mossy shoreline, scrawny brown mushrooms were pushing through the fall's cover of dead leaves where a rotting log was providing a field day for ants and other insects. All the while, the lush green trees quivered in the lazy breeze.

With a crackling of twigs, a long fly fishing rod was thrust out from behind a bush. A tall, thin fisherman followed close behind, and almost fell as he crossed over the marshy grasses. The fisherman stretched out a little line and started to cast. After a few casts, a nine pound rainbow trout darted out from under a rock, heading straight for the cast fly. As the fish reached the fly, the water boiled behind him, but he suddenly turned and shot back to the rock's safety.

This continued for about twenty minutes, until on one cast, the fish rocketed through the water, taking the fly with him. After a long struggle, the fisherman pulled the exhausted fish to a net. The fisherman held up his glittering trophy, the nine pound trout, but seeing what a beautiful fish it was, he decided to release his catch.

The fish quivered in the water for a few seconds, and then, slowly but smoothly swam back to his home under the rock. Meanwhile, the fisherman secured his line, put his creel over his shoulder and stumbled away through the lush vegetation. In a few minutes he returned, having forgotten a small plastic tackle box. As he again left the stream, he first got his fishing rod tangled in a tree, and then dropped his tackle box, and generally left the fishing spot in a much less graceful manner than the fish had.

– by Jamie

After graduating from the Rudolf Steiner High School in New York City, Jamie attended Stanford where he studied English and biology, then spent some time at Oxford University, where he studied English, ran cross-country and sang in a choir. He has his masters degree in marine biology from Northeastern University and is presently working on his doctorate in marine biology at Stanford.

CHAPTER 3

WISH

By the time we get to the second of our three weeks, we hope to have achieved a certain depth of mood through our rigorous approach. Nevertheless, were we to give unpremeditated writing exercises about wishes, many of the resulting wishes would be shallow. So once again, we must engineer the depth. We must ennoble these wishes, make them worthy, golden wishes, wishes not to be squandered. Wish, is, after all, potent, and can be used for good or ill, as so many of the fairy tales show us.

Let us recall the hierarchy of will in which wish has its rightful place. We find it in *The Study of Man*, Chapter 4:

instinct
impulse
desire

motive
wish
intention
resolution

We are dealing here with volition, the realm of the will, with what leads into the future.

By illuminating WISH we can provide the seventh graders with a moment in which ideals may be articulated. If the seventh grader is guided to articulate noble wishes, to cast a beacon into the future toward which the soul can knowingly or unknowingly continue to steer, immeasurable depths of soul may be discovered. The student will experience the flashing up of a higher self. Often, however, such an evaluation must come from the teacher. The students themselves are likely to think nothing of the most extraordinarily lofty wishes. The wishes will not be lofty, however, unless we support the golden possibilities.

There are some marvelous biographies in which a child's wish (or dream, as this sort of wish is sometimes called) determines the destiny of an individual. Heinrich Schliemann, the discoverer of Troy, comes to mind. The wish to discover the ancient city of Troy arose in him after his father had read stories to him about the fabled city. Young Heinrich wanted more than anything to find the lost city. To achieve his goal, he had to amass lots of money, and in order to do that, he had to learn many languages, and he did both so well, that he soon had the fortune he needed, as well as the knowledge required, to begin a series of explorations. Eventually, he did discover the site of ancient Troy.

Explorers, athletes, scientists, artists, all sorts of people have achieved outstanding successes because of childhood wishes. Such "dreams" may turn out to be very real indeed. Think of Albert Schweitzer, for instance.

If, on the first day of the WISH week, you bring in some such biography, and you then ask the children to write a composition for you in which they describe a wish that they have, you will not have to add any warning words about avoiding petty or crazy wishes. You will have set the mood of reverence in wish. Still, if you want to get a good composition, you might consider giving the class an outline for its first WISH composition, thereby providing them with the essential structure. Such an outline can be quite vague:

1. State the wish.
2. Describe in detail what you would do if the wish were granted.
3. Conclusion: why do you think this is an important wish?

Then, for the rest of the week, many other kinds of wishes can be considered:

- a wish for someone else
- a wish the class makes together
- a wish for the earth
- a fairy tale type of wish
- a wish for the future
- how I wish to improve myself
- a story in which a wish plays a crucial role
- fulfilling someone else's wish
- "If I could...."
- "If I had...."

The more integrated the entire week is, the more thorough the mood you can establish. Just remember, all this has to be happening on a seventh grade level. There has to be plenty of blue in the mix, otherwise the children will rebel. So you must work hard on the *science* of the writing itself. That is the marvelous secret of this main lesson block. The content is truly compelling; *if* properly harnessed, it will not lead to never-never land. Instead, it will carry you and your class into hitherto unapproachable realms of soul experience. I say "hitherto unapproachable," because hitherto the children were still entirely *in* this soul realm, and thus could not approach it, and now that they can begin to approach such depths, they *will* not approach it unless coaxed. But in the seventh graders, "The wishes of the soul are springing" already, and already, "life grows more radiant...more arduous...more abundant...." Seventh grade souls are longing (wishing) for an excuse to be serious. That is part of the explanation for their frenetic behavior; it is a masquerade. Under the masks of silly, rowdy, gnawing behavior, is a soul, in need of something filling, something grand. Your weakest writers may reveal astonishing depths of soul under the influence of a *scientifically* conceived incentive.

IF I HAD....

[with original spelling and punctuation]

If I hade a time machine I would go back in time to when Adam and Eve lived. I would pretend I was one of their people I would stay ontil I was jus about born. All thes millons and millons of years would seem like only a few years. The reason I would want to go back in time is I'm curious about what they did and what they looked like.

– by Patrick

IF I COULD....

If I could talk to the animals I would become famous. If I got bored I would go and play with the animals. I would make a little store for them. If an animal got hurt I would ask him to tell me what happened and fix it. If an animal got lost it would tell me where they lived and I would bring it home. If I were in trouble I would tell an animal to get help. If I hade to milk a cow I would talk to her while I was doing it. I would soon build an animal hospital. I would never be afraid of animals when I walk in the forest.

– also by Patrick

UNDER THE SEA

If I had a chance, I would walk under the sea for a day. [long list of what he would see....]

I should like to see the bottom of the sea, where no man has ever been before, and where there would be a rest from all of the upper world.

– by Aram

Patrick was a dreamy boy, blond, broad-shouldered, the oldest of four brothers, a student who struggled. He was a seventh grader at the Great Barrington Rudolf Steiner School in rural Massachusetts. He did not attend a Waldorf High School. He pursued cross-country skiing, at which he was very good.

After graduating from the Rudolf Steiner School in New York City, Aram pursued his interest in writing, language, theater. He graduated from Columbia with a major in history and is presently a journalist in New York City.

What measureless inner depths both boys plumbed when they wrote their homework compositions on WISH. What are they remembering? What are they seeing? What are they looking toward?

From Aram's class, here is one last example. It comes from that class's eighth grade physiology block, all about the muscles and the bones. In class, we had had a preparatory conversation, but the substance of the essay is the writer's own.

ESSAY ON WILL, DESIRE, INSTINCT

Will is a powerful muscle. Yet it is not in the body. It is used to decide something, to make a decision, to make up your mind. For instance, if you wake up in the morning earlier than usual, and it is cold outside, you do not want to get up. You would prefer to stay in your nice warm comfortable bed. It takes a lot of will to get up and decide to go out in the cold, and then do it. However, it is not at all easy. It is easy to decide, but to actually do it is a lot harder. If you are walking along and you see an ice cream cone store you might walk in. You would tell yourself to walk in, you would not do it instinctively.

Instinct is a subconscious will. You do not decide to do something, you just do it without even thinking about it. If someone throws something at your eyes, they will shut to protect themselves. You do not decide to shut them at all, you do not even think about shutting them, but they shut anyway. Your body knows that you have to do it and it does it. When a baby is born, it starts to breathe. Nobody teaches it how, it just knows and that is what instinct is. To subconsciously do the right thing.

Desire is to want something. It can be sometimes very dangerous. A robber steals because of his desire of money or jewels or whatever type of a thief he happens to be. If you become thirsty you desire something to drink. Your desire to be something can make you go to great lengths to fulfill your desire. If your desire is to be a doctor, you have to do a lot of work. Most of the time, you do not want to do this work but you do, because of your desire to be a success.

These three qualities (or faults, as the case may be) belong to every human being. However, every person has a different will, desire or instinct, which helps to make us all different. And that is the way it should be.

– by Christian

Were this a high school essay, we could fault it in many ways. The older the student, the sharper our analysis would have to be. But this is an eighth grader's work. It reveals the struggle for clarity of thought, as well as the magnitude of the step that can be taken between seventh and eighth grade. Were Christian's eighth grade thoughts partially affected by his seventh grade main lesson on "WISH, WONDER AND SURPRISE?" Possibly.

Christian attended law school at UC Berkeley and now practices law in San Francisco.

CHAPTER 4

SURPRISE

We can be pleasantly surprised, but we can also be surprised to death, literally. Unpleasant news that comes all of a sudden, unpleasant events that happen unexpectedly, can cause the heart to falter. If the shock is big enough, the heart may stop beating. If the pleasant surprise is big enough, we might call it a miracle. The gamut of SURPRISE is broad, ranging in scope from a surprise, which, once we have gotten used to it, addresses our deepest sympathy, to one which is so antipathetic that we excarnate entirely. Initially, however, any surprise, small or great, lifts us out of ourselves. We may be lifted out just a little bit, hardly aware of the surprise; we may be jolted, and experience the adrenaline rush which helps us stay in our bodies; we may lift out entirely. The gradations are infinite. But what they all have in common is the excarnating effect of surprise.

What is the value in precipitating this effect? Perhaps it will be helpful if we substitute "amazement" for "surprise." Amazement is surprise with the added element of awe. Amazement is an ennobled form of surprise. What are the benefits of amazement?

The element of surprise that underlies amazement lifts us out of ourselves, while the element of wonder in amazement allows something new to stream in. Amazement, with its nuance of shock, provides us with the opportunity to change our minds, our opinions, our assertions. For seventh graders, whose opinions are frequently vehement and obdurate, guided practice in meeting the unexpected is salubrious. The seventh grade soul may discover the benefit of the unexpected, may discover the *golden* opportunity in adapting to the unexpected.

So take your class by surprise! Give them a genuine, enjoyable, unpredictable, inexplicable surprise. Break the routine, but beware lest you get too far out, for then it will take days to collect all the seventh graders into their own skins again. Avoid anything that smacks too much of a practical joke. For seventh graders, "surprise" may well mean little more than "practical joke." And although a practical joke **is** a surprise, it sets a better example if your surprise is genuinely funny, without the aggression that often lurks in the practical joke. All humor depends on the element of surprise. When we laugh we are expressing, by exhaling, some shock, small though it may be. So if, with your surprise, you make the children laugh, that's just fine.

Should you decide to surprise them by, say, disguising yourself, simply do it. Do not talk about it, analyze it, explain it. Or there may be an unexpected visitor or happening in the classroom that day. Just let it be. Just give them the experience, and let the suspense around the event build. Even the next day, you need not return to the subject of yesterday's "event." Let the surprise **be.**

For the rest of the week, the challenge is: how to keep the surprises from becoming predictable. Again, it is important to focus on the writing. It will be easier to immerse the children in the mood of SURPRISE if you have managed to avoid calling the main lesson block "Wish, Wonder and Surprise." You may want to plan one or two more surprises for the seventh grade. How wonderful it would be if a clown could visit the class.

But there is also the possibility of the surprise that is experienced in the imagination. For example, you might ask the students to write a surprise ending to a short story you read to them. It could be a mystery, for what better master of the unexpected than Sherlock Holmes? Unfortunately, the detective genre is fraught with unsavory characters, so you might find it advantageous to make up a mystery story of your own, one suited to the class, the school, the locale. Instead of providing the ending, ask the students to devise one of their own. Give them some guidelines: the ending must come out of the story itself; it must be a surprise; one new character may be introduced....

Other possible SURPRISE actions:

• Have the class plan a surprise for another class, or for the school. Ask the students to write up *Surprise Proposals.*

• Games: write one sentence, pass the paper on. This will work better if you give specific indications of what should be in the first sentence, the second, etc. For example:

1. Introduce the main character.
2. Describe the character.
3. Describe the setting.
4. Give detail of the setting.
5. Introduce an animal.

And so forth.

• Compositions: about finding something unexpected; about doing something unexpected; about doing something that someone else didn't expect. And so forth.

• Work with a short story by O'Henry, the master of surprise endings.

At the end of this main lesson block, the children should feel that they have *learned* something about writing, the way they *learned* something about the human body in physiology.

Fundamental to all this learning is the mood of soul we tried to create in our first week: wonder. Wonder is the hidden force in the Waldorf curriculum. Earlier in this article, we encountered wonder as the basis of cognition. In the first chapter of *The World of the Senses and the World of the Spirit*, Rudolf Steiner develops wonder as the basis for knowledge.

"All knowledge must have wonder as its seed." All knowledge that does not start with wonder, "leads merely to an acquaintance with truth that may be compared with making a plant of papier-mâché and not raising it from a seed. The comparison is quite apt! For all real knowledge that hopes to have a chance of coming to grips with the riddles of the world must grow out of the seed of wonder....A thinking set in motion without the condition of wonder remains nothing but a mere play of thought. All true thinking must originate in the mood of wonder." [6]

Rudolf Steiner then develops three further moods of soul which will lead the human being to truth: wonder leads to reverence, then to wisdom-filled harmony, then to surrender, and finally to truth.

CHAPTER 5

CONCLUSION

In a different set of lectures, *The Spiritual Foundation of Morality*, the investigation concludes with WONDER in the final chapter. And here WONDER is directly connected to the other two soul moods of our seventh grade block.

> All philosophical thought begins with wonder.... Something essentially moral is said when we say that our relationship to the supersensible world begins with wonder. The savage, uncultivated human being is but little affected by the great phenomena of the world. It is through mental development that man comes to find riddles in the phenomena of everyday life, and to perceive that there is something spiritual at the back of them. It is wonder that directs our soul up to the

> spiritual sphere in order that we may penetrate to the knowledge of that world; and we can only arrive at this knowledge when our soul is attracted by the phenomena which it is possible to investigate. It is this attraction which gives rise to wonder, astonishment and faith. It is always wonder and amazement which direct us to what is supersensible, and at the same time, it is what one usually describes as faith. **FAITH, WONDER AND AMAZEMENT are the three forces of the soul which lead us beyond the ordinary world**. [Emphasis added.][7]

Here, then, we have perhaps the broadest possible basis for our seventh grade main lesson. We do not want to lead the children into the supersensible, at least not directly. Our immediate goal is that they may "penetrate," in a manner appropriate to their age, "the knowledge of the world." We want the seventh graders' souls to be "attracted by the phenomena [of everyday life]." If we manage to encourage this attraction, by cultivating FAITH, WONDER and AMAZEMENT, then the likelihood of destructive attractions is lessened.

That would be a profound and compelling reason for "Wish, Wonder and Surprise" in the seventh grade. But there is a larger context. And although the magnitude of active wonder, as Rudolf Steiner develops it in these lectures, extends far beyond the purview of seventh graders or of this article, for the Waldorf teacher it is necessary to acknowledge the cosmic basis of the curriculum:

"Wonder," states Rudolf Steiner, "only appeared in evolution in the age when the Christ-impulse had come into the world ... after supersensible wisdom had disappeared."

We might say wonder infuses the blue sky just as the golden sky disappears.

Rudolf Steiner then describes how "wonder and amazement" lead to brotherhood, which leads to truthfulness. In turn, truth leads to knowledge of the supersensible and "through knowledge we shall attain to the supersensible wisdom which has already sunk into the subconscious depths of the soul."

Furthermore, "through all **moral activities** [emphasis added], all acts performed as the result of wonder, trust, reverence and faith, in short, all that paves the way to supersensible knowledge, we form [something which closes like a covering round the Christ, something comparable to the astral body of man] the astral body for the Christ-Ego-impulse."

Such then, is the mighty realm out of which the golden light shines not only into the seventh grade main lesson called, "Wish, Wonder and Surprise," but also into the lesson preparation of the Waldorf teacher.

POSTSCRIPT

For my own introduction to the potential of this approach, I am indebted to my high school English teacher at the Rudolf Steiner School in New York City, Christy Barnes. When I was a twelfth grader, she gave us a sequence of assignments asking us to describe various aspects of light. Her focus was the **way** we did this. Were we using too many adjectives and adverbs and not enough nouns? Then we had to write a story. And, lo, our stories, influenced by the Russian writers we had studied, though still nominally about the outwardly perceptible phenomena of dark and light and the precise vocabulary needed to describe it, expressed depths of our own souls which we would never have known about, let alone have revealed, had our own souls been the focus of attention.

With gratitude for my own experiences first as a Waldorf high school pupil, then as a Waldorf class and high school teacher, I hope this in-depth study of one grade in particular can help inspire English teachers of all grades.

ENDNOTES

1. For elucidation of the term, see Neil Postman's exemplary book, ***Technopoly, the Surrender of Culture to Technology*** (New York: Vintage Books, 1992).

2. Steiner, Rudolf , ***Knowledge of the Higher Worlds and Its Attainment*** (Hudson, N.Y.: Anthroposophic Press, 1947), p. 12.

3. Steiner, Rudolf , ***Practical Advice to Teachers*** (London: Rudolf Steiner Press, 1976), p. 125.

4. Steiner, Rudolf , ***Knowledge of the Higher Worlds, and Its Attainment*** (Hudson, N.Y.: Anthroposophic Press, 1947), p. 13.

5. Steiner, Rudolf , ***Cosmic Memory, Prehistory of Earth and Man***, second edition (W. Nyack, N.Y.: Steiner Publications, Inc., 1959), pp. 226-227.

6. Steiner, Rudolf , ***The World of the Senses and the World of the Spirit*** (North Vancouver, Canada: Steiner Book Centre, 1979), pp. 6-7.

7. Steiner, Rudolf , ***The Spiritual Foundation of Morality*** (North Vancouver, Canada: Steiner Book Centre, publication date not listed), pp. 80-90.